The Stanzas of time

A poetry collection inspired by everyday life

Copyright © Palak Tewary, 2023

The author asserts the moral right under the Copyright, Designs and Patents Act 1988 to be identified as the author of this work

All Right Reserved. No part of this publication may be reproduced, stored in a retrieval system or transmitted, in any form or by any means without the prior consent of the author, nor be otherwise circulated in any form of binding or cover other than that which it is published, with the exception of certain activities permitted by applicable copyright laws, such as brief quotations in the context of a review or academic work

Publisher: Powerful Thoughts

Dedication

*To Ma, Pa & Princess
for always believing in me*

Contents

A glimpse of me...in honesty 11

A place called Home 12

A Strange Collection 13

A symphony of destiny 14

Acceptance 16

Ambition 17

An incomprehensible walk-through life 18

An uninvited guest 19

Boredom 20

City in my mind 21

Defining me 22

Discovery 23

Each day 24

Favourite colour 25

Greatest fear 26

In a moment 28

In the Desert 29

Insight 30

Let her dreams fly 31

Lifemates 32

Love 33

Masks	34
Meetings	35
Memories never forgotten	36
My tribe	37
On life's path...	38
Pride	39
Reborn	40
Reflections	41
Resurrection	43
Secrets	44
To be a child again	45
Understanding the unspoken language	46
Unintended Course	47
Wanderer	48
Within a box	49
Different forms of poetry explained	51
Blank Verse Poem	52
Couplets	53
Free Verse Poem	54
Glose/Glosa Poem	55
Haiku Poem	56
Palindrome Poem	57
Prose Poem	58

- Pentastich Poem...59
- Rhyming Poetry...60
- Shakespearean Sonnet...................................61
- Terza Rima Poem..62
- Trenta Sei Poem..63
- Triversen Poem..64
- Villanella Poem..65

Guess the poetry form..67
The Poems and their forms................................71
About the Author...75

A glimpse of me...in honesty

A glimpse of me you can see
in my books sitting on my shelves
in the mementos I collect in my memory box
a glimpse of me you can see
in the value system of my family
and in the company that I keep
a glimpse of me you can see
in the stories written on the paths I have walked
also, in the chaotic footprints I have left behind
a glimpse of me you can see
in the clouds that float past each day retelling my yarn
in the stars that write my coming destiny
a glimpse of me you can see
in my ancestors' presence that still lingers on
and in the ruins of my old home
a glimpse of me you can see
within every conversation I have had
and through every facade that I have built
and in all these glimpses
perhaps you can finally see me
honestly

A place called Home

(First published on placesofpoetry.org.uk)

No, I do not belong here
There is another place that is home
And since I have never been there
I can say, it isn't Rotterdam or Rome

It looks like a page from a favourite book
That has come alive at my behest
With secrets to discover in every nook
And a quench for every quest

It feels like silk at every step
Nay-a-blister to be seen
Where instead of air, there is pep
Which makes me dance like a queen

No, I do not belong here
There is another place that is home
To find it, I need no seer
Just a bit of a dream honeycomb

A Strange Collection

(First published on Pen to Print: 2nd Place - Poetry Competition'21)

I collect hearts – broken hearts. In horror, you jump a mile from me and look at me aghast. Yes, it sounds awful, doesn't it? It may be a trying tale to tell but tell I must. For this cannot be hidden, you know. I collect broken hearts. Truth be told, its not as easy as it may sound – for, though there are many that are and remain broken, not many are willing to trade them away. They keep them holding tight in their fist, as if it was gold that I had asked for. Or they try to hide it from sight, so sometimes it's difficult to know its there. Or they try and convince me that it is not shattered at all – simply bruised. Mayhap, they are trying to persuade themselves? I collect broken hearts. Even though it's not as easy as it sounds. Rummaging deep (sometimes), I find there are incalculable amounts to add to my collection. In every corner. In every junction. On every street. At every meet. And though they all come from different places, they all look the same. Crimson. Shiny. Broken. I collect broken hearts. You may ask what I trade in return. That's where the magic is, my friend. They can choose what they want. Listening ear. Shoulder to cry on. Someone to sympathise. Empathy galore. Laughter to share. Burden to bear. Someone to understand. A helping hand. A friend indeed. A hug that they need. Perchance, my story you shall share and foraging for my compendium may become easier. Tell them, I collect broken hearts.

A symphony of destiny

Deep within, a voice does dwell,
Its echoes reach from heart to soul,
A force that speaks, with tales to tell,
A melody that makes us whole.
It sings of joy, it sings of pain,
Of love that blossoms, like a rose in rain,

Its echoes reach from heart to soul,
Of triumphs won, and shed tears.
It hums of all parts that make us whole,
It sings of dreams, it sings of fears,
It speaks in whispers, soft and low,
Or booms with strength, a mighty flow,

A force that speaks, with tales to tell,
It lulls us with a soothing hum,
Or boldly shouts, loud as bell
Or rattles us, like a thundering drum,
It calms our doubts, it clears our minds,
Or sparks rebellion, the fire that binds.

A melody that makes us whole.
It knows our essence, knows our core,
It guides us; mind, body and soul,
And leads us to our inner shore.
It's not just words, it's not just sound,
But a symphony that can astound,

It sings of joy, it sings of pain,
So, listen close, and heed its call,
To rise above the challenges, conquer the bane,
For it's the voice that tells us all,
The melody of highs and lows, disclosed,
From birth to death, our lives composed,

Of love that blossoms, like a rose in rain,
And as we play our part upon life's stage,
To find the deeper meaning, the lessons to retain,
With each new measure, we turn the page,
Through struggles, we find strength to strive,
In symphony of destiny, we're alive.

Acceptance

(First published on Write On! Extra – Pen to Print)

Cuddled up on the window seat,
one lazy sunny beautiful afternoon,
with me, I am determined to meet

The pale sunray falls into the saloon,
and lights up the shadowed places,
and fills it with a delightful sweet tune

The wind caresses the lost spaces,
letting the air breathe and hum with
songs of forgotten stories and faces

I decode my own magic and myth,
revisiting the pathways that I chose,
unlocking doors without the locksmith

Absolving myself, many a chapters I close,
albeit with thorns I may be, but I am a rose

Ambition

In the silence of the night,
Listening to my increasing heartbeat,
And thus, of my aim, I gain sight,
Contemplating the mammoth feat

In the quest of a flaming desire,
Pumping adrenaline into my veins,
And so, burning with fever, I feel on fire,
Mulling over the forward terrains

In short, I sit here, for my heart's goal,
Seeking the next steps to take,
And hence, assessing the expected toll,
Planning the potential stake

An incomprehensible walk-through life

(First published on https://floodlightpoetry.wixsite.com)

On a crimson pillow of clouds,
a motorless car leaves behind
a cold trail of unanswerable questions;
Does god exist? What's after death?
A bulbul emanates and sings to me,
a glimpse of music so profound, that
in this temporary world,
I yearn for perseverance,
moving through every stage of life,
with specs firmly attached,
I yearn for perseverance,
in this temporary world.
A glimpse of music so profound that,
a bulbul emanates and sings to me.
Does god exist? What's after death?
A cold trail of unanswerable questions,
a motorless car leaves behind,
on a crimson pillow of clouds.

An uninvited guest

The wind knocked ferociously on the window
demanding to be let in, before it fell ill
perhaps, it was too cold outside
but didn't it know, it was the one causing the chill?

Silently trying to creep
through the tiny little gaps, it could find
to heat itself against the warm tender radiators
leaving a cold smoky trail behind

Asking to be housed tonight
it whimpered slowly up to me, as if in lieu
of an absent cuddle but I, made of sterner stuff,
wrapped the duvet closer and bid the wind adieu

Boredom

I have counted the steps it takes
From the kitchen to the bedroom
And then again from the bedroom to the door
Eighty-seven and twenty-four

I have rearranged all the furniture
And then put it back as before
In case you don't find it nifty
I did however take photos – a hundred and fifty

I painted all the walls blue
And then since they matched my mood
I turned them all to green
Perhaps, doing it once more, may lose its sheen?

City in my mind

It was different, this city that I had walked into there was a moon that was made of water that swam across the cobbled lanes, filling each house with a liquid light house that were made of flowers and diamonds, where everyone was treated just the same it was different, this city that I had walked into its lanes were made of glass where you could walk up-side-down and see reflections of living dreams and nightmares, but none were eroded or snatched it was different, this city that I had walked into where every fear was manifested into a violet-eyed monster (the only criminal that you had to fear) that stayed by your side until you began to become unafraid of your own fears it was different, this city that I had walked into where every aspiration you had, flowed out of you into rivers of chocolate and chilli – the taste of which was surprising and oh! so tempting - which no one could take away from you it was different, this city that I had walked into where trees bore fruits that were called kindness and trust and friendship and acceptance that could be collected in all seasons where weeds of hate and malice and felony and wrong didn't exist it was different, this city that I had walked into its citizens were as pure as air that lives above the clouds and its air was as pure as the love a dog feels for its master alas, it was different, this city that I had woken into!

Defining me

Through the fog of life, I could not see
What I was truly meant to be
I tried – I really tried to scale mountains
And suffered numerous terrains

I walked the lone walk
Alone and proud, until I came to a deadlock
The fire within unextinguished
The path, unwillingly, relinquished

I crashed against the rocks life threw
The marks left me a little subdue
I joined the herd, flung my hat in the ring
But I was like a caged songbird, unable to sing

Left limp, scattered everywhere
It finally dawned, I didn't have to declare
I, yes, I – don't have to be one thing
I could be all – or anything

Discovery

The sound of silence,
empty streets and empty parks
making loud noises

The palpitations
of the heart, uneasily
finding joy in self

Each day

I try to start every new day,
with spirits bright and gay
However, by night, I find myself sunken low,
trying to get over the day's blow

Have I not woken up from a bad dream,
that makes me noiselessly scream?
Or is this a brutal reality check,
that makes me into a colossal wreck?

Weary, I have bawled my eyes out,
alone, of course, - with not a soul about
I, then join, reluctantly, the land of the living
and find myself with a head – that is splitting!

Eager, I try to free my tortured soul,
but I suspect I am losing all control
Mayhap it be my imprudent doggedness,
however, my same struggle tomorrow shall witness

Favourite colour

(First published on palaktewary.com)

the pink and orange hue of the sunset;
or the white and blue of the cloudless sky;
maybe the green of the swaying leaves in the breeze;
also, the yellow of the shining sun;
perhaps the brown of my father's eye as they twinkle at me;
and the red of my mother's lips as she laughs at my antics;
it could be the black in my sister's hair that I see as she hugs me;
or the gold in my grandmother's watch that flickers in front of me, as she raises her hands to bless me;
probably the grey and silver of the moonlit night;
even the purple and navy of bruises attained in the quest of an adventure;
almost certainly the spectrum in the rainbow;
and its probable its the one in a blooming flower;
how do I choose but one colour?

Greatest fear

Ghosts that dance in the hall
Noises which torment every night
Shadows clinging on every wall
Doubts that take away the light
Something I cannot even see
An icy dark fear clutches me

Noises which torment every night
Of neighbours party loud and heavy
Are more annoyance than fright
And making complaints is petty
So, finding sound sleep buds
Should stem the flow of noise floods

Shadows clinging on every wall
Of all kinds of sizes and shapes
Made of my imaginative scrawl
Even spread onto the drapes
But disappear as darkness spreads
Leaving me free of all dreads

Doubts that take away the light
Squeezing every ounce of spirit
Until there is only a dull white
Swallowing all and every merit
Can make my heart thump
And cause a frightening jump

Something I cannot even see
Unless I stand in front of the mirror
When the eyes tell me to flee
And expression makes it clearer
That all that frightens me, is I
Wrenching from me a desolate sigh

An icy dark fear clutches me
There seems to be no escape
I must now cease to be
And bear a different cape
To free my pitiable soul
Before doubt takes its toll

In a moment

(First published in Emery Arts Anthology)
Based on Art piece: Light House (Two of each kind)
https://www.emeryarts.org/artists-a-j/frank-cole

Deep cerulean ocean, as far as the eye can see
A sunlit bright afternoon, filling the heart with glee

The singing of the sky, carrying notes of white clouds
Far and above - away from every and all crowds

Gleaming rays on the naughty dancing waves
That crash, quivering against the coral caves

A sudden sharp gloom dampening the bright
The warning realised from the house of light

In but an instant, the smoke of darkness gathers
And the shallow fickle happiness, the storm shatters

In the Desert

Night glowers, its darkness closing in,
and yet, a strange light accompanies,
with the thousand stars lighting up the way.

The hot humid air, that still feels warm,
burns into the skin,
soaking the clothes in sweat.

The silence, louder than any noise heard,
drowns all thoughts and thoughts,
leaving behind a strange calmness.

The shimmering mirages play a teasing, sly
trick on wandering souls, as the hot winds sigh,
echoing the isolation that makes one's heart awry.

The coarse sand, under the feet,
feels like bath salt stuck at the bottom,
cleansing and pure, removing everything dead within.

In the desert's embrace, under the burning eye,
find the strength to endure, to strive and fly,
for even in desolation, life finds a way to comply.

Insight

Amidst the chaos of life's daily grind,
A voice whispers softly from within,
Guiding with wisdom, gentle and kind.

In solitude, when thoughts are akin,
The inner voice echoes with clarity,
A compass, a beacon, a guiding spin.

It speaks in hushed tones with sincerity,
Urging caution when temptations call,
Or cheering on with unwavering authenticity.

Through trials and triumphs, big and small,
The inner voice serves as a faithful guide,
A compass that leads, standing tall.

In moments of doubt, it will not hide,
But offers counsel, profound and deep,
With intuitions that help us to decide.

Though often ignored in the noisy sweep
Of external clamours, it remains true,
Patiently waiting, a treasure to keep.

So, harken to the whispers, let them ensue,
For within you, lies a beacon, forever anew.

Let her dreams fly

(First published on palaktewary.com)

Let her dreams fly
Give her a chance, don't deny

There are barriers and there is bias
But these can be shattered by us

So, let's make a change, you & I
And let her dreams fly

Lifemates

After a graceful flight across hundred
miles with unhurried wingbeats and
outstretched necks, they land gently.

In the silken folds of the glistening water
the two swans come together like no one
else exists in their realm of the world.

Softly bending their heads towards the
other they breathe in the sweet scent of
eternity amidst the smooth tributary.

Entwining their necks with one another
to form one heart, they swim to fables
of bonds that last throughout life.

Representing Viveka where they
take us, mere mortals, through the
galleries of the eternal and transient.

Loyally, they live amid the golden sands
of time, to determine new revered
paths in sync alongside each other.

Love

(First published on palaktewary.com)

In darkness, a glimmer of light;
In mind, even if not in sight;
In every heart, maybe even in every beat;
At every corner and every street;
There is Love, there is Love

His flower, and her ring;
The music in life, that makes you sing;
A smile to cherish,
A tear to perish,
That is Love, that is Love

Holding Grandmother's hand;
Hanging on to father's shoulders rather than stand;
Mother's touch on the forehead;
Sisters' bonhomie where all worries are shed;
It is Love, it is Love

A friend's shoulder to lean on;
Sitting alone in the lawn;
A finger to lead you;
Matters not; when, where, how or who;
All is Love, all is Love

Masks

In the sanctuary of my room
I take it off, the facade that I have worn all day
I must adorn another one soon
Even to just go down the hallway

I savour, these few moments
Touching my cheeks in awe
My eyes reflecting my truth
Where I am the only law

It's getting trickier
To find these few seconds unmasked
I must get better at crushing my spirit
If they knew – alas, they would be aghast

Hiding in plain sight
I fear I may forget
The face that I am meant to be
The one concealed, with regret

I know I am not the only one who disguises
Knowing that – doesn't make it any easier
If each one of us had the courage to show
Perhaps life would be dreamier

But no one takes the first step
As we each battle our own demon
And lose ourselves within our masquerades
Hoping someone, someday, will be a beacon

Meetings

(First published in Explore York anthology)

Handshake, roundtables,
pats on the back and squeezing
in just one more chair
...no news!

Half-chic appearance
on a little window in
a thirteen-inch screen
...strange indeed!

Memories never forgotten

It was the sight, that I have never forgotten,
of the clear, translucent water in the lake
in the midst of the mountains, where
I had first learnt swimming strokes

It was the taste, that I have never forgotten,
of the honied, tangy, succulent mulberries
straight off the trees, that
I had first climbed stealthily to get

It was the feel, that I have never forgotten
of the hard, unbreakable brick wall
that found itself in the middle of my face, when
I had first been pushed in a game

It was the sound, that I have never forgotten
of the waves colliding against the rocks
by the exquisite cerulean sea, as
I had first built sand castles and dreams

My tribe

It is not just a place where I grew up
or the neighbourhoods where I made friends
it's that sense of belonging that I carry along
wherever I go, I know I am not alone
my tribe comes with me

It is not about being able to resolve problems
or chat about issues over cups of tea
it's that spirit that makes me proud of
whoever I may be, as I embody values
my tribe instilled in me

It is not about numbers that determines
the strength of the community
it's that willingness to give back in
whatever way I can, to ensure that
my tribe strengthens via me

On life's path...

In the midst of the night,
In the glare of the afternoon,
An inane fear grips my heart
My heartbeat thunders with no rhyme nor tune

Why does it all feel so uncertain?
Why are all directions so blurred?
Is it the mist in my eyes or the fog on the road,
That my path hasn't turned out as I augured?

Is it a series of challenges or is it a game of hurdles?
Or is life, a number of unanswered questions?
At some point – we all must stop and ask,
The reason and results of our actions

Pride

Strong and proud, I stood
Refusing to back down
A promise made; consequences understood
No matter the result, there shall be no frown

Strong and proud, I may look
To the third eye that gazed
They didn't hear the tremor in the voice that shook
If they had, they would have been amazed

Strong and proud, I wait
Even though I have heard that pride comes before fall
And it may yet be my biggest mistake
But for my pride, I have staked it all

No matter what results I shall see
Strong and proud, I shall always be

Reborn

(Adapted from the poem first published on Write On! Extra – Pen to Print)

There is something light in this dark
A wave of paradise within a melancholy night
Perchance a misguided star left its mark

There rises a definite slow-burning spark
Winking from the scorching wood of my pyre
There is something light in this dark

In the silent realm where dreams disembark
The soul burns with newfound desires
Perchance a misguided star left its mark

Now at the dusk of time, happy as a lark
Leaving a trail of stardust in this cosmic mire,
There is something light in this dark.

A glorious new journey, I now embark
Unbound from every earthly sacrament
Perchance a misguided star left its mark

Waking into a new birth with a start
I soar on the faint shimmering air
There is something light in this dark
Perchance a misguided star left its mark

Reflections

(First published on Write On! Extra – Pen to Print)

In the centre of my home,
I find there is an immense blue,
that fills with my essence with glee
as the voices of the open terrain
echo against the blank walls,
telling yarns, they had seen in awry
footsteps of travellers that walked
through the same trail, before me;
the reflections, as clear as the sky,
they flash upon that inward eye.

The air was as pure as the love
of a mother for her child and
the water that cascaded from
the peak as translucent as the
spirit of a being that had attained
nirvana. As the journey renewed
inside the mind space, I reached
Elysium, where I was the lone
and distinct victor, an attitude
which is the bliss of solitude.

Within the barriers of my confined
chair, where I only have the recall
of expanse pieces of heavens, the
strong arms of the vast Himalayas
cradle me in my despair, and when
I close my eyes, I can feel the chills
of the cool ether against my hot skin,
calming my unease in our man-made
cage, with phenomenal unseen skills
and then my heart, with pleasure, fills.

As I step into the garden, for
my piece of land under the
clouds, I find that it is within
my grasp, no matter where I am
to bring the mountains to me.
I call to the protector of the hills
and the seas and carry myself
into me to the locale I was the
happiest and my glum soul stills
and dances with the daffodils.

Resurrection

(Adapted from the poem first published in Emery Arts Anthology)
Based on Art piece: A Phantasmal Peace, 2014,
https://www.emeryarts.org/artists-s-z/susan-scot

Out of the ashes she glows,
fiercer and brighter than before,
just like how the phoenix rose.

Her frozen courage, unfroze,
to pool into a liquid fire and
out of the ashes she glows.

With each trial life bestows,
her power and resolve soar,
just like how the phoenix rose.

In the cauldron of life, she knows,
each test, a chance ultimate and
out of the ashes she glows.

As surely as the wind blows,
she will soar to heights new,
just like how the phoenix rose.

A fierce spirit, her light flows
in the darkest of dark hours,
out of the ashes she glows,
just like how the phoenix rose.

Secrets

They swirl all around me
teasing and furtive
following insistently
asking me, daringly, to set them free
to roam the earth

I take one out of the cold air, randomly
and take a peek, stealthily –
lest anyone else fathoms
the hidden miserable tale

Shaken, I set it back
losing it quickly amongst
the whirling, alluring enigmas
that constantly mock

Feigning them a make-believe
I snub them; these invisible hefty
unbreakable cage of secrets that
follows doggedly; laying in my path, eternally

To be a child again

(Adapted from the poem first published on palaktewary.com)
Inspired by my favourite Ghazal "Wo kagaz ki kasti"

Days of Disney cartoons, cakes and cherries,
Nights full of stories of trolls and fairies,
And how do I forget the paper boats and rain,
Oh…to be a child again

The higher the swings, the louder the laughter & screams,
Content with the collection of hopes and dreams,
When wealth was dolls, marbles and a wooden train,
Oh…to be a child again

Happiness was receiving and sending parcels,
Or going to the sea and building sand castles,
Or even just catching sight of an aeroplane,
Oh…to be a child again

Worry meant fights with friends & making up once more,
And learning the timetables for eight, twelve and four,
And mayhap seeking those hiding – from lane to lane,
Oh…to be a child again

Tapestry of life, woven in colours bright
Innocence a-plenty, the world felt right
Every moment full of wonders to gain
Oh…to be a child again

Now, when those times have gone, memories stay
Sweet nostalgia keeps the hearts blithe and gay
And deep down inside, that child still remains
So…to be a child again, free yourself from chains

Understanding the unspoken language

A pat on the back
– did it mean approval or was it an act of comfort?
A rub on the arm
– an indication for familiarity or a display of sympathy or maybe it's just a show of complacency?
An all-embracing hug
– a want for closeness or a demand for reassurance?
An arm over the shoulder
– is it protectiveness or perhaps, possessiveness?
Holding a hand
– to guide, to connect or to lead?
Arm in arm
– friendship or security?
Tuck of the hair behind an ear –
is it care or is it despair?
Resting head against shoulder
– because of weariness or ease?
The conundrum called touch
– silent, unstated, tacit
– so easily misunderstood or unacknowledged
Be careful!

Unintended Course

A complicated progress along life's road
over tortuous terrains; escaped – unharmed? Upon
leaving behind a myriad of steps,
that shall tell the story of a life lived unlived,
across numerous unchartered pathways,
alongside countless unchosen guises,
to become unrecognisable to oneself,
wondering if the cost is worth it? Certainly,
to become unrecognisable to oneself,
alongside countless unchosen guises,
across numerous unchartered pathways,
that shall tell the story of a life lived unlived
leaving behind a myriad of steps
over tortuous terrain, escaped – unharmed upon
a complicated progress along life's road.

Wanderer

It's not just a hobby, but a calling
A calling of the land beyond that beckons
That beckons and pulls at the strings of my heart
My heart that awaits a new place and its dawn

It's not just a hobby, but a passion
A passion for learning, for finding and for understanding
For understanding the nuances of our personas
Our personas that form the very nature of our world being

It's not just a hobby, but a way of life
A way of life that shows the path of fulfilment
Of fulfilment and enlightenment and realisation
Realisation of self and self-accomplishment

Within a box

Confined and labelled within a box
In a space so narrow, so unkind but
I am more than their limited thoughts

They judge and they design, like it unlocks
Who I am but they can't see past the mould
Confined and labelled within a box

But I won't resign myself to their talks
I am not a copy nor a cliché; I am unique
I am more than their limited thoughts

I will find the way to walk my own blocks
To break free from the unrefined display
Confined and labelled within a box

I am inimitable, a treasure that shocks
Those who won't listen, won't take in that
I am more than their limited thoughts

Let them define and let them knock
I will keep shining my light beyond for
I am more than their limited thoughts
Confined and labelled within a box

Different forms of poetry explained

Poetry conveys a thought, a story, an idea in a lyrical arrangement of words. There are many ways to structure poems with lines and meters and syllables and beats and stanzas. It can also be freeform with no structure. These are just a few types of forms explained, which are used in this poetry book.

Blank Verse Poem

Blank Verse Poems are poems with a precise meter called iambic pentameter – but that does not rhyme.

This means that each line contains five iambs – two syllable pairs where the second syllable is more pronounced / emphasized.

Couplets

A couplet is made up of two consecutive poetry lines that create an idea or thought.

These have similar syllabic pattern called a meter. Most couplets tend to rhyme, but not all do.

These can be within a larger poem or be a poem on its own.

Free Verse Poem

Free verse poems tend to lack a consistent pattern, scheme, rhyme, metre or musical form.

They are not devoid of structure but there is a lot of leeway allowed when composing a free verse poem, especially when compared to other poetry forms which are stricter such as black verse.

Glose/Glosa Poem

The glose or glosa is a Spanish form. It has the below features:

- Quote four lines from another poem or poet as an epigraph
- These lines act as a refrain in the final line of the four stanzas written by the poet – so, first line would be final line of first stanza, second line ends the second stanza and so forth
- Most common convention are that each stanza are 10 lines in length
- Line length is usually set by the epigraph

Haiku Poem

A Japanese poetry form, Haiku, is made of short unrhymed lines that conjure natural imagery.

It can come in various formats of short verses but the most common is a three-line poem with a syllable pattern of five-seven-five.

Palindrome Poem

A palindrome is a word or phrase that reads the same backward and forward.

Palindrome poems, also known as mirrored poems, use line palindromes within a poetic form.

They begin with an initial poem and then feature a line at the halfway mark that reverses the rest of the lines in order.

Prose Poem

Prose poetry combines elements of lyrical and metre of a traditional poetry along with language of prose like punctuation, lack of line breaks etc.

There is no fixed definition of prose poetry however it may include elements such as:

- repetition
- resonance
- a metrical or rhythmic structure
- soft or hard rhymes
- metaphors
- figures of speeches

etc.

Pentastich Poem

Pentastich poems consist of stanzas or poem of five lines.

They are often also known as cinquain or quintet.

Rhyming Poetry

This sort of poetry forms a rhyme scheme that repeats at the end of a line or stanza. The schemes can change line by line, stanza by stanza, or can continue throughout a poem.

Poems with rhyme schemes are generally written in formal verse, which has a strict meter: a repeating pattern of stressed and unstressed syllables.

The design is fixed by letters of the alphabet. Lines elected with the same letter rhyme with each other. For example, the rhyme scheme ABAB means the first and third lines of a stanza, or the "A"s, rhyme with each other, and the second line rhymes with the fourth line, or the "B"s rhyme together.

There are various types of schemes such as:

- Alternate rhyme - ABAB
- Ballade – ABABBCBC
- Coupled rhyme - AABB
- Enclosed rhyme – ABBA
- Simple four-line rhyme – ABCB

Etc.

The beauty about this type of poetry is that you can have any type of scheme you like.

Shakespearean Sonnet

A variation of Italian sonnets, this form of poetry includes the following elements:

- Fourteen lines long
- Divided into four subgroups – The first three subgroups have four lines each which makes them "quatrains," with the second and fourth lines of each group containing rhyming words
- The sonnet then concludes with a two-line subgroup, and these two lines rhyme with each other
- There are typically ten syllables per line, which are phrased in iambic pentameter

Terza Rima Poem

A rhyming verse form, consisting of:

- tercets (three-line stanzas)
- with an interlocking three-line rhyme scheme where last word of second line in one tercet provides rhyme for the first and third lines in tercet that follows i.e., aba bcb cdc ded ee
- The poem ends with either a single line or a couplet that rhymes with previous tercets's middle line.

Trenta Sei Poem

These are a 36-line poem which have a rhyme pattern and refrain as follows:

- There are six sestets i.e., six-line stanzas
- Each sestet has ababcc rhyme pattern
- Each line in the first stanza makes the first line in the corresponding stanza i.e., line 1 is the first line in first stanza, line 2 is first line in second stanza etc.

Triversen Poem

These are an 18-line poem made up of:

- Three-line stanzas
- Each stanza equals one sentence.
- Each line is a separate phrase in the sentence
- There is a variable foot of 2-4 beats per line.
- There should be six stanzas

Villanella Poem

This is a poetic form that has 19 lines and uses repeated lines and a strict rhyming pattern.

There is a lyrical quality to this type of poem with their structured lines.

A type of poem with:
- total of six stanzas
- five three-line stanzas that follow a rhyme scheme of ABA
- the first and third lines of the first stanza repeat in the following stanzas at the end alternately
- the villanelle concludes with a four-line stanza with the pattern ABAA

Guess the poetry form

Can you guess which poem was written using which form?

1) A glimpse of me…in honesty
2) A place called Home
3) A Strange Collection
4) A symphony of destiny
5) Acceptance
6) Ambition
7) An incomprehensible walk-through life
8) An uninvited guest
9) Boredom
10) City in my mind
11) Defining me
12) Discovery
13) Each day
14) Favourite colour
15) Greatest fear
16) In a moment
17) In the Desert
18) Insight
19) Let her dreams fly
20) Lifemates

21) Love

22) Masks

23) Meetings

24) Memories never forgotten

25) My tribe

26) On life's path...

27) Pride

28) Reborn

29) Reflections

30) Resurrection

31) Secrets

32) To be a child again

33) Understanding the unspoken language

34) Unintended Course

35) Wanderer

36) Within a box

The Poems and their forms

*This list of all poems and
the form used to construct them*

1) A glimpse of me…in honesty ~ **Free Verse Poem**

2) A place called Home ~ **Rhymed Poem - ABAB**

3) A Strange Collection ~ **Free Verse Poem**

4) A symphony of destiny ~ **Trenta Sei Poem**

5) Acceptance ~ **Terza Rima Poem**

6) Ambition ~ **Rhymed Poem - ABAB**

7) An incomprehensible walk-through life ~ **Palindrome Poem**

8) An uninvited guest ~ **Rhymed Poem – ABCB**

9) Boredom ~ **Rhymed Poem – ABCC**

10) City in my mind ~ **Free Verse Poem**

11) Defining me ~ **Rhymed Poem - AABB**

12) Discovery ~ **Haiku Poem (set of 2 Haikus)**

13) Each day ~ **Rhymed Poem – AABB**

14) Favourite colour ~ **Free Verse Poem**

15) Greatest fear ~ **Trenta Sei Poem**

16) In a moment ~ **Couplets**

17) In the Desert ~ **Triversen Poem**

18) Insight ~ **Terza Rima Poem**

19) Let her dreams fly ~ **Couplets**

20) Lifemates ~ **Triversen Poem**

21) Love ~ **Rhymed Poem - AABBC**

22) Masks ~ **Rhymed Poem - ABCB**

23) Meetings ~ **Haiku Poem (set of 2 Haikus)**

24) Memories never forgotten ~ **Blank Verse Poem**

25) My tribe ~ **Pentastich Poem**

26) On life's path... ~ **Rhymed Poem – ABCB**

27) Pride ~ **Shakepearean Sonnets**

28) Reborn ~ **Villanella Poem**

29) Reflections ~ **Glosa/Glose Poem – using Wordsworth's Daffodil's last 4 lines**

30) Resurrection ~ **Villanella Poem**

31) Secrets ~ **Blank Verse Poem**

32) To be a child again ~ **Rhymed Poem - AABB**

33) Understanding the unspoken language ~ **Prose Poem**

34) Unintended Course ~ **Palindrome Poem**

35) Wanderer ~ **Rhymed Poem - ABCB**

36) Within a box ~ **Villanella Poem**

About the Author

Palak Tewary

An Indian-born Londoner, is a management and finance professional, who along with being an ardent writer, is a travel buff and a photography and videography enthusiast.

She writes on travel, books, photography, business and motivation as well as poetry and fiction. She is inspired from everyday life and her work leans towards trying to provide positivity, happiness and encouragement or to inspire thoughtful consideration on social issues and self-development.

She blogs at **www.palaktewary.com** which also features her fiction, non-fiction and poetry work – including that published on various platforms.

Connect with her on:
YouTube / Twitter/X / Instagram: **@palaktewary**

   Visit her **amazon page**

www.ingramcontent.com/pod-product-compliance
Lightning Source LLC
Chambersburg PA
CBHW071318080526
44587CB00018B/3268